PUFFIN BOOKS

BITS AND CHIPS
How a Computer Works

It's great fun to play games on a computer, but have you thought just how many other things are done by computer? It's the fact that they can be instructed to do a great number of things that makes computers different from other machines.

This book clearly and memorably outlines how these amazing machines work. And it describes simple activities that vividly demonstrate the principles of how, for example, a keyboard converts letters into signals that the computer can process, or how information is stored on a disc.

Written and illustrated in a lively and enjoyable style, this original and stimulating introduction to computers is sure to give you a sound basic understanding of one of the most important machines in the modern world.

Neil Ardley, winner of the 1989 Science Book Prize and *The Times Educational Supplement* Information Book Award, is the author of many books for children on science subjects. Being a keen musician and composer, he has also written on music. He lives in Derbyshire.

Also by Neil Ardley

Snap Happy – how a camera takes pictures
Tune In – how TV and radio work
Wings and Things – how an aircraft flies

Neil Ardley

CHIPS

How a Computer Works

Illustrated by
David Woodroffe

PUFFIN BOOKS

Consultant: Andrew Nahum, Curator of
Aviation, The Science Museum, London

PUFFIN BOOKS

Published by the Penguin Group
Penguin Books Ltd, 27 Wrights Lane, London W8 5TZ, England
Penguin Books USA Inc., 375 Hudson Street, New York, New York 10014, USA
Penguin Books Australia Ltd, Ringwood, Victoria, Australia
Penguin Books Canada Ltd, 10 Alcorn Avenue, Toronto, Ontario, Canada M4V 3B2
Penguin Books (NZ) Ltd, 182–190 Wairau Road, Auckland 10, New Zealand

Penguin Books Ltd, Registered Offices: Harmondsworth, Middlesex, England

First published 1991
10 9 8 7 6 5 4 3 2

The moral right of the author has been asserted

Printed in England by Clays Ltd, St Ives plc
Filmset in Linotron Melior

CONTENTS

Note to readers:

Every effort has been made to ensure that the
instructions for the activities in this book are clear
and safe. None the less, every care must be taken in
the use of such items as scissors and electrical
appliances. Care must also be exercised in
performing the activities to ensure that injury or
damage is not caused. Children must seek adult
supervision before attempting these activities.

CHAPTER 1

CLEVER MACHINES

The computer is a very special kind of machine. All the other machines that we use can do just one job. A camera takes pictures and a radio makes sound, for example. But a computer can do many different things. It can work out sums at lightning speed; it can play games; it can teach you things; it can make music. A computer can also store vast amounts of information, like the titles and authors of all the books that people can buy. It can then instantly give us any piece of information from its huge store. Computers can even speak to us, and they are beginning to be able to understand human speech. They really do seem to be very clever machines.

What makes the computer so different from every other type of machine? It is able to do all kinds of different tasks because the computer can be given instructions. It has a memory that remembers these instructions, and the computer follows them to perform a task. We can give it different instructions so that it will carry out different tasks. People write the instructions, and it is their instructions that are clever rather than the computer itself.

COUNTING UP

Do you remember how you learned to count with your fingers? You could add up two numbers by moving your fingers for each number. Then you counted the total number of fingers that you moved.

It may seem strange, but a computer works rather like this. It does everything by counting numbers, even when it is playing games or making music. Instead of moving fingers, it shifts electricity at high speed. The computer handles the numbers very, very quickly, and

can do millions of sums in just one second. It would take your fingers several years to do all the sums that a computer can do in a second! In that time, you would almost certainly make a mistake. But the computer does all its millions of sums and almost never makes a mistake.

ADDING UP WITHOUT SLIPPING UP

Counting on your fingers is slow and it's easy to make a mistake. How much better to have something that can do sums for us. It will do them quickly and get the right answer. The computer is not the only kind of counting-machine. You can make a very simple adding-machine with a piece of paper. Rule a line across the paper. Use a ruler to mark centimetres along the line and number them as shown. Then cut the piece of paper into two strips along the line. Place the two strips together.

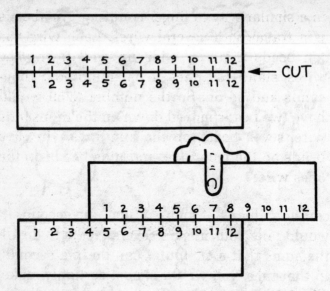

Suppose you want to add 4 and 7. Slide the top strip so that its end is opposite 4 on the bottom strip. Then see which number on the bottom strip is opposite 7. It is 11, and this is the answer: $4 + 7 = 11$. This simple adding-machine is easy to use and it is always right. People used a similar device called a slide-rule to do sums until pocket calculators were invented. The calculator is a kind of small computer that only does sums.

ANCIENT ADDER

The computer in fact grew out of a long line of counting-machines. About 5000 years ago, people invented a very good device to add numbers. It is called the abacus, and it works in a similar way to finger-counting. An abacus is a frame with several wires. Each wire has ten beads that can slide up and down. The wires stand for ones, tens, hundreds, thousands and so on. So the number 2759 would have two beads moved down on the thousands wire, seven beads on the hundreds wire, five beads on the tens wire, and nine beads on the ones wire.

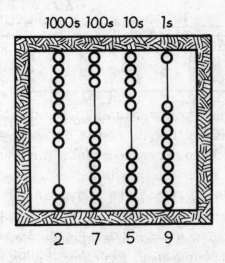

You add numbers with an abacus by moving beads down the wires for each of the numbers. There's only one rule: if all ten beads move down any wire, you must then move all the ten beads back up the wire, and move down one bead on the next wire. Provided that you move the right amounts of beads, the correct answer will appear on the abacus.

HOW TO ADD 163 AND 356 WITH AN ABACUS

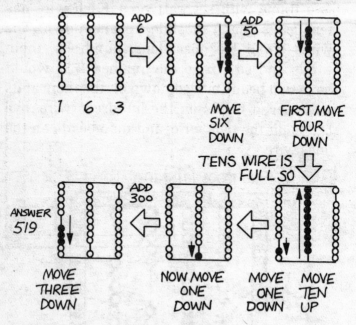

CARDBOARD CALCULATOR

Calculators display actual figures, so they are easier to use than the abacus. Before computers, people used mechanical calculators to add numbers. These calculators had moving parts, unlike the electrical parts inside computers and today's calculators. Cash registers in shops may still work in this way.

You can make a good calculator from two cardboard boxes. Follow the instructions given on page 13. You feed the numbers into the calculator by using a pencil to move the

YOU WILL NEED TWO IDENTICAL
WASHING POWDER BOXES—
1·05 kg SIZE (23cm × 16cm × 6cm)
IS IDEAL. CUT A SIDE FROM
ONE BOX, CUT THE CORNERS
AND FOLD BACK THE SIDES.
STICK THEM WITH TAPE.

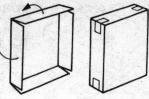

NOW DRAW THREE
WINDOWS IN THE
POSITIONS SHOWN
AND CUT THEM
OUT ———————→

ON THE SIDE YOU
HAVE CUT OUT
DRAW THESE TWO
WHEELS AND CUT
THEM OUT. MAKE
HOLES IN THEIR
MIDDLES WITH A
DRAWING PIN

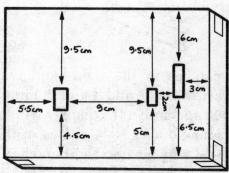

WRITE NUMBERS ON THE WHEELS
AS HERE—

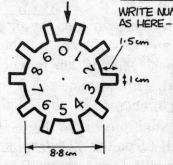

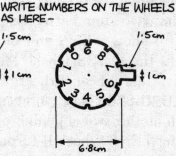

TAKE THE SECOND
BOX AND MAKE
TWO HOLES WITH
A DRAWING PIN
IN THE POSITIONS
SHOWN

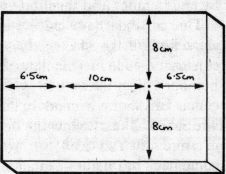

CONTINUED ON
NEXT PAGE —

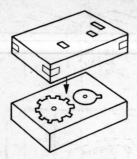

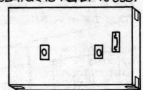

BEND THE TEETH ON THE WHEELS DOWN SLIGHTLY, THEN PIN THEM INTO POSITION. PLACE THE FIRST BOX DOWN OVER THE WHEELS AND YOUR CALCULATOR IS READY TO USE.

notches in the right-hand window with the arrow. Let's add 4 and 8. First make sure that 00 appears in the display windows. Then move four notches – 04 shows in the display. Now add 8 by moving eight notches. The answer 12 comes up in the display.

The two number-wheels inside the calculator show TENS and ONES. The notches are in the ONES wheel. Moving ten notches makes this wheel turn around once. As 9 on the ONES display changes to 0, the single tooth on this wheel pushes one of the ten teeth on the TENS wheel. It turns the TENS wheel by one number and the total goes up by 10.

The cardboard calculator adds up in the same kind of way as the abacus. Both of them can carry one, just as you do when adding numbers. When a column of figures in a sum comes to 13, say, you write down 3 and carry one on to the next column of figures. The computer also works by carrying one, and we'll come back to this in Chapter 8.

CHAPTER 2
INS AND OUTS

*C*omputers are easy to use – almost as easy as talking to someone. We can give words and numbers to the computer by pressing keys, and the computer's screen can display messages for us or results, such as scores in a game. A computer printer can write information or draw pictures for us to keep. Although the computer may seem able to read and write, it does not work with words in the same way as we do. It handles words – and everything else, such as numbers, pictures and music – in the form of electric code signals.

The computer is not like a spy. Its code is not a secret code, but it is hard for people to understand. For us to make use of the computer, it must have parts that can change the numbers and letters we use into code signals. It also needs other parts to change the computer's code back into our numbers and letters.

These parts are called the input units and output units. They allow us to use the computer. It is through these units that the computer is able to work for us. We 'talk' to the computer with its input unit, and it 'talks' back to us with its output unit. The keyboard of a computer is an input unit. Pressing a key with a certain number or letter sends a code signal for that number or letter into the computer. The screen is an output unit, and so is a computer printer. These output units change the computer's code back into the numbers and letters that we understand.

THE KEYS TO THE COMPUTER

Each key in the keyboard of a computer is an electric switch. Under the keys are rows of wires or metal strips. When you press a key, it connects a pair of wires or strips together. An electric current flows along the pair of wires or strips to a microchip inside the computer. Microchips are small electronic devices with

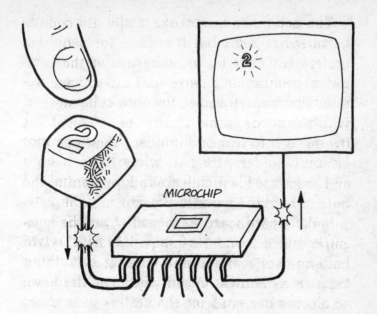

rows of metal 'legs' that make them look like oblong caterpillars. The legs connect the microchip to wires that go to the other parts of the computer, such as the keyboard.

Microchips are like tiny electronic brains. They produce and handle the computer's code signals. Electric signals enter and leave the microchip through its legs. When you press a key, a microchip gets an electric current along a certain pair of wires or strips. It then produces the code signal for the key that is pressed. Each key in the computer keyboard connects a different pair of wires to the microchip. Each pair makes the microchip produce a different code signal.

You can make a working model of a simple keyboard to see how it works. You'll need a battery, two torch bulbs, some cardboard, aluminium cooking foil, wire and nine drawing-pins. The battery and bulbs should be marked with about the same number of volts (V). Fit the bulbs into two bulb-holders. If you cannot get bulb-holders, fix two wires to each bulb and put some Plasticine around the base of the bulb to hold the wires in place.

Make a cardboard keyboard with four keys marked 0, 1, 2 and 3 as shown. Mark the two bulb-holders 1 and 2, and connect everything together as shown. When you press the keys, an electric current from the battery goes along the wires to light the bulbs. The bulbs should light to show a number. Pressing key 3 makes bulb 2 and bulb 1 light: $2 + 1 = 3$. Pressing key 2 makes only bulb 2 light, whereas key 1 makes bulb 1 light. Key 0 makes neither bulb light. If the bulbs do not light correctly, the connections are probably loose.

The bulbs light with a code for the numbers. It's a very simple code; all you do is say whether bulb 2 and bulb 1 are on or off. Three is on-on, two is on-off, one is off-on, and zero is off-off. This kind of on-off code is called binary code, and all computers use it. We'll return to binary code in Chapter 7.

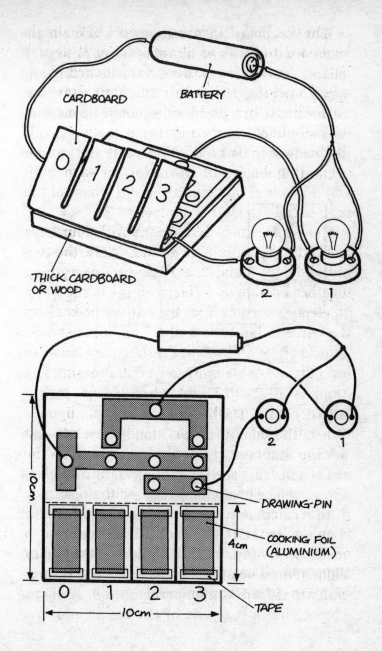

CARDBOARD

BATTERY

THICK CARDBOARD
OR WOOD

2 1

DRAWING-PIN

COOKING FOIL
(ALUMINIUM)

TAPE

0 1 2 3

10cm

10cm

4cm

The keyboard in a computer works in the same kind of way as our simple set of keys. It changes not only numbers, but also letters and signs into electric signals in on-off code. The connections are much more complicated than in our simple keyboard. From the keyboard, the code signals go to other parts in the computer that work with the codes.

SEVEN AT A TIME

When the computer has done its work, like adding numbers, it produces a code signal for the result. This goes to the output unit, such as the screen or printer, and we see the result.

In a calculator, the screen is a liquid crystal display, or LCD for short. Each numeral is made of seven bars in a pattern like a figure eight. The seven bars go dark or light in patterns that form the numerals 0 to 9. A microchip changes the code of the result into new

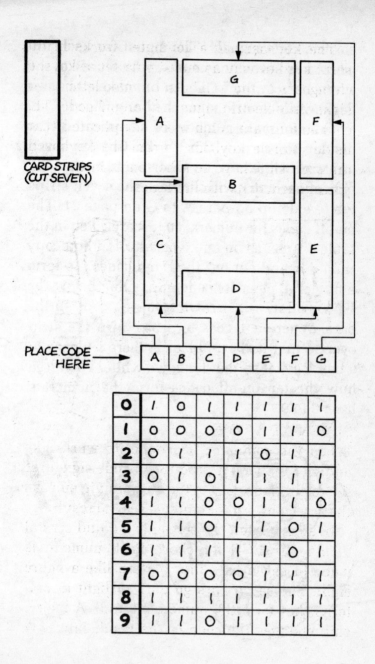

CARD STRIPS
(CUT SEVEN)

PLACE CODE
HERE

	A	B	C	D	E	F	G
0	1	0	1	1	1	1	1
1	0	0	0	0	1	1	0
2	0	1	1	1	0	1	1
3	0	1	0	1	1	1	1
4	1	1	0	0	1	1	0
5	1	1	0	1	1	0	1
6	1	1	1	1	1	0	1
7	0	0	0	0	1	1	1
8	1	1	1	1	1	1	1
9	1	1	0	1	1	1	1

21

electric code signals. The signal for each numeral has seven ons or offs, which control the seven bars in the LCD. An on makes a bar go dark, while an off makes the bar go light.

You can make a model of a numeral in the display to see how this works. Cut out seven strips of white card as shown, and colour one side of each strip black. Place the seven strips white side up on bars A to G on page 21. The on-off codes for numerals 0 to 9 are given in the table – 1 means on and 0 means off. Photocopy the table and cut out these ten codes. To form a numeral, place its code in position below the bars. Follow the arrows from the code to the bars. Where a 1 goes to a bar, turn the strip over so that it shows black. Where a 0 goes to a bar, leave it so that it shows white. You'll see how the ten on-off codes form the numerals from 0 to 9.

GOING DOTTY

The letters and numbers that appear on a computer screen are made in a similar way. The screen works like a television set. Instead of seven strips, rows of tiny dots light up or go dark to form each number or letter. Computer printers called dot-matrix printers print rows of dots in the same way. On-off code signals go to the screen or printer. Each on in the code forms a dot, while each off gives a blank. The dots form patterns that we see as numbers and letters.

Here are five sets of blank dots (shown as circles), and five sets of on-off codes:

10001	11111	10000	10000	01110
10001	10001	10000	10000	10001
10001	10000	10000	10000	10001
11111	11110	10000	10000	10001
10001	10000	10000	10000	10001
10001	10001	10001	10001	10001
10001	11111	11111	11111	01110

Each set has five columns of seven dots each. Using the five sets of codes, fill in each blank dot that has an on (1) in its code. A word will appear, just as it would on a computer screen or printer. In fact, computer screens and printers use more dots than this to form letters, numbers and signs that look sharp and clear.

CHAPTER 3

PLAYING WITH PICTURES

*C*omputers can do much more than work out sums with numbers and display messages in writing. When we play a computer game, we often see a moving picture on the screen. We can press keys on the keyboard and things happen to the picture. Computer pictures are called computer graphics. How is the computer able to produce and change pictures?

PAINTING BY NUMBERS

Take a magnifying glass and look closely at a picture on a computer screen. You'll see that it is made of lots and lots of tiny squares. Each square is called a pixel, which stands for picture cell. Some of the pixels light up, often in different colours. When you look at the screen from a normal distance, the tiny pixels merge together to form a picture.

The computer is still a counting-machine, even though it can display pictures. The on-off codes that it uses are, in fact, codes for numbers, and it 'thinks' of the picture as a set of numbers. It does this by giving three numbers to each pixel – two position numbers and one colour number. The first number gives the position of the pixel across the screen, the second

number its position down the screen, and the third number gives the pixel its colour. The computer sends thousands of code-numbers to the screen, which instantly changes them into a whole picture.

You can see how this works by colouring the set of squares below. These would be 64 pixels on a screen – just a small part of a picture. Colour 2 is red and colour 3 is green. All the other squares stay white.

Use these codes to form the picture:

4,1,2 (4 across, 1 down, colour 2)

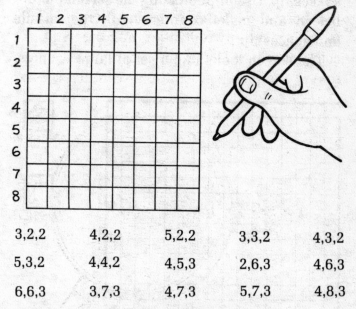

3,2,2	4,2,2	5,2,2	3,3,2	4,3,2
5,3,2	4,4,2	4,5,3	2,6,3	4,6,3
6,6,3	3,7,3	4,7,3	5,7,3	4,8,3

Colour in the squares and you should get a red flower with a green stem and leaves. In the same way, the computer would light up these pixels in red and green to show a small flower.

The computer can change the picture just by changing the pixel numbers. Altering the position numbers can make something move to a different place on the screen, and changing the colour numbers gives it a different colour. A whole set of new numbers gives a new picture.

PLAYING THE GAME

Let's see how the computer can play a simple game in which you have to aim a missile at a spaceship. Use or photocopy the screen picture below, and make counters with the missile and spaceship.

The screen looks like a set of large squares,

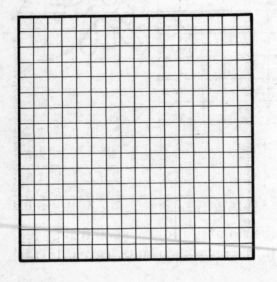

SPACESHIP

MISSILE

which is how the computer divides up the picture. Each square contains enough pixels to form a picture of the spaceship or missile. The computer changes their position numbers so that the spaceship flies across the screen at any level, moving one square at a time. It also makes the missile move up the screen, one square at a time as well.

The computer starts the game by placing the spaceship at one side of the screen and near the top. Using the keyboard or another unit called a joystick, the player places the missile anywhere along the bottom of the picture and fires it. The computer now takes over. It changes the position numbers to move the spaceship across one square and the missile up

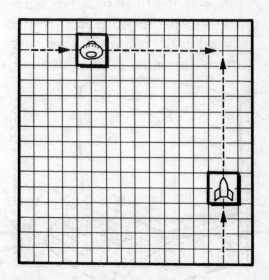

one square. It does this alternately. Move the spaceship and missile one after the other to see what happens. If they both arrive on the same square, then a hit is scored. The computer knows if this happens because the position numbers of the spaceship and missile will be the same. It then adds up the score and starts again.

A MOUSE IN THE HOUSE

Many home computers have a mouse, but it's not a little furry animal. The mouse is another kind of input unit that works the computer instead of a keyboard, and it's very easy to use. You can give commands to the computer with the mouse, and make the computer do things that are impossible with a keyboard. The screen may display the commands as several little pictures called icons. Each one stands for some kind of action. An icon of a

dustbin, for example, means that you can get rid of some information in the computer. A paintbrush means that you can use the mouse to paint a picture.

You move the mouse with one hand, and an arrow moves over the screen in the same direction as the mouse. Move the arrow to an icon, and then press a switch on the mouse. The computer then obeys the command shown in the icon. After switching on the paintbrush, you can then 'paint' by moving the mouse. A picture will build up on the screen as if you were handling a brush.

The mouse contains a ball that rolls as you move the mouse. Parts rotate inside the mouse, which sends out code signals to the computer. These change the position numbers of the arrow so that it follows the direction of the mouse. As the arrow moves over the screen, the computer keeps track of the arrow's position numbers. It also knows the position numbers of the various icons on the screen. When the arrow reaches an icon, its position numbers and the icon's position numbers will be the same. This is how the computer can tell which icon you choose with the mouse.

You can play a game of Treasure Hunt to see how the mouse is used. Photocopy the picture on page 32 and paste it to some cardboard. The picture is a computer screen full of icons.

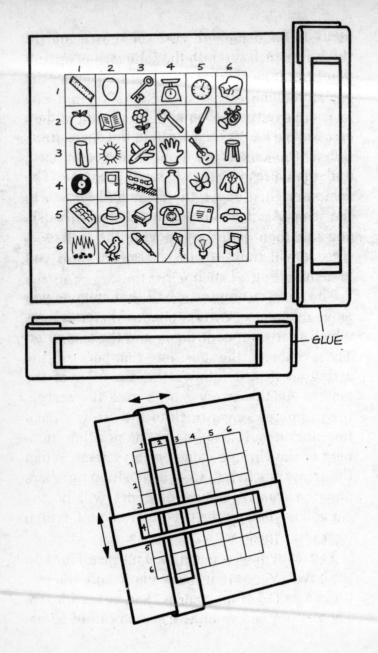

GLUE

Make the sliders with card as shown and fit them over the screen so that one moves up and down, and the other moves across. To play the game, you move the card-sliders so that one icon appears in the square where the sliders cross. This is like choosing an icon with a mouse. Then note the number at the top and the number at the side of the sliders; these are the icon's position numbers.

You start at the door. Find its position number (2,4) and look them up in the table. You'll get a clue – 'Open the door with it'. Go to another icon that answers the clue, such as the key, or maybe the axe. Its position numbers will give you another clue. Solve this clue to find the next icon, and continue until you find the treasure.

Position	Clue
1,1	It lights up.
1,2	It keeps you warm.
1,3	You can write with it.
1,4	It's in the room.
1,5	You can measure with it.
1,6	It's got hands.
2,1	It can fly.
2,2	You can put it on your head.
2,3	You talk into it.
2,4	Open the door with it.
2,5	You can blow it.

2,6	It breaks easily.
3,1	You can eat it.
3,2	What's the time?
3,3	You can wear it.
3,4	You can sit on it.
3,5	It's got wings.
3,6	It could have your name on it.
4,1	It can sing.
4,2	You can travel in it.
4,3	You can shake it.
4,4	It has a message for you.
4,5	You can listen to it.
4,6	It grows.
5,1	You could play with it.
5,2	It's bright.
5,3	It's made of paper.
5,4	It's found on trees.
5,5	It contains the treasure – you've won!
5,6	It's got legs.
6,1	You can read it.
6,2	You can drink it.
6,3	It's got arms.
6,4	How heavy are you?
6,5	It makes music.
6,6	It might smell nice.

CHAPTER 4

MAMMOTH MEMORY

SO THAT'S HOW IT NEVER FORGETS!

*T*here's a saying that an elephant never forgets, so it must have a mammoth memory. A computer is good at remembering things too. It can remember information like names and addresses, how much money you save, the score in a game or the spelling of words. It can also remember the instructions that make it perform a certain task, like playing a game or word processing. The computer remembers all these things with its memory.

In fact, the memory of a computer is a main unit like the input unit and output unit. The input unit puts information into the computer, like numbers to be added. The memory stores the instructions, such as how to add up. The computer contains a microchip called a processor that follows the instructions to add the numbers, and produces the result. The output unit shows the result, and the memory can also store the result. This is basically how all computers work.

WHAT DO YOU KNOW?

A computer has two main kinds of memory units. The first kind is rather like your own memory, which is in your brain. Your memory contains things that you always know, like being able to speak English. It also contains things that you remember only for a while, like the time you are going to do something today or tomorrow. You'll never forget how to speak, but you soon forget things like times, which you do not need to remember for long.

Inside the computer are several microchips (or chips) that contain its memory. One kind of memory chip stores instructions and information that the computer always needs in order to work, like the shapes of the letters of the alphabet. This kind of memory is called ROM, which stands for Read-Only Memory. The computer does not forget the instructions and information in ROM, just as you do not forget how to write the letters of the alphabet.

The other kind of memory chip is called RAM, which stands for Random-Access

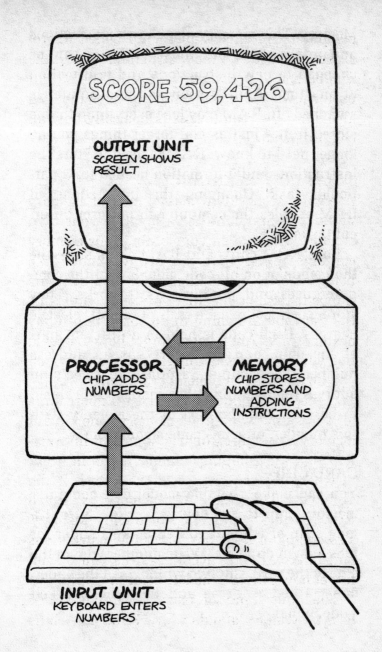

SCORE 59,426

OUTPUT UNIT
SCREEN SHOWS
RESULT

PROCESSOR
CHIP ADDS
NUMBERS

MEMORY
CHIP STORES
NUMBERS AND
ADDING
INSTRUCTIONS

INPUT UNIT
KEYBOARD ENTERS
NUMBERS

Memory. This memory also stores instructions and information, but those in RAM can be changed to new instructions and information at any time. And as soon as the computer is switched off, RAM may lose everything that is stored in it – just as you forget things you no longer need to know. RAM is used to store the instructions and information needed for a particular task. Changing the instructions in RAM enables the computer to perform different tasks.

Both ROM chips and RAM chips store the thousands of on-off code signals that the computer uses and produces as it works. They store each code as a set of on-off electric charges. Each code is held in a different part of the chip, and each part has an address number. The computer's processor selects an address number and either sends a code signal to be stored at the part of the memory with this number, or gets a code signal from it.

CARD CHIP

You can make a simple model of a computer memory chip to see how it works. Cut out a long strip of white card and make a slider for it as shown opposite. Write numbers down the side of the card. Cut two windows in the slider, one marked Address and the other marked Code Signal.

To see how the chip works, move the slider up and down the card. Address numbers appear in the small window. The code signal at each address can be written or read in the big window. Use 1 for on and O for off. In a ROM chip, the codes would be written in ink so that they are not lost. In a RAM chip, the codes would be written in pencil so that they can be rubbed out and new codes written in. In fact, computer people talk about 'reading'

the memory to get information from it, and 'writing' the memory to store information.

A memory chip is tiny – about as big as a zero written on your card chip. Yet it can store millions of on-off charges.

MAGNETIC MEMORY

Some computers have batteries, such as portable computers that people carry around with them. These may keep their RAM chips powered up so that they do not lose information when the computer is switched off. But many computers do need a second kind of memory unit to store information and instructions that are lost when they are switched off. It's rather like writing down things that you need to know at some time but cannot keep in your memory – such as cooking recipes and lists of ingredients. A second memory unit is also important because it can store many different sets of instructions and information. This unit will store much more than the computer's RAM, which generally holds only one set at a time.

The second memory unit is a disc-drive or a tape-player. It is a separate unit that you connect to the computer, or it is built into the computer. The unit gets electric code signals from the computer's processor, and turns them into magnetic signals on a magnetic disc or

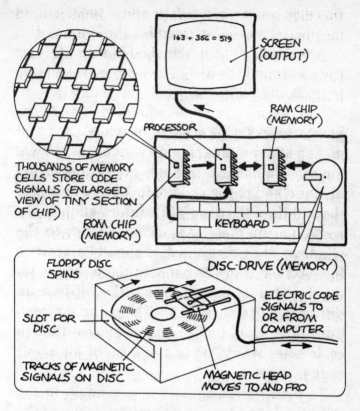

SCREEN (OUTPUT)

163 + 356 = 519

RAM CHIP (MEMORY)

PROCESSOR

THOUSANDS OF MEMORY CELLS STORE CODE SIGNALS (ENLARGED VIEW OF TINY SECTION OF CHIP)

ROM CHIP (MEMORY)

KEYBOARD

DISC-DRIVE (MEMORY)

FLOPPY DISC SPINS

ELECTRIC CODE SIGNALS TO OR FROM COMPUTER

SLOT FOR DISC

TRACKS OF MAGNETIC SIGNALS ON DISC

MAGNETIC HEAD MOVES TO AND FRO

tape. Magnets have north and south poles, and the on-off electric code signals become magnetic signals in which the magnetism is either north or south. Discs store huge amounts of information. You can easily hold several small computer discs in one hand. Yet each one can store enough code signals for writing that would fill several books as printed letters.

Inside a disc-drive, a magnetic head moves across the disc between the centre and edge.

The disc rotates beneath or above the head. As the disc turns, the head sends signals to the disc or gets signals from it. The signals are in circular tracks around the disc. The head moves to and fro to find a particular track very quickly.

You can make a model of a disc-drive to see how it works. Cut a circle of white card and make a slider with a moving window as shown. Push a matchstick through the centre of the disc and end of the slider. Move the window to the middle of the disc. Write information, like a name, on the disc by marking a letter in the window. Then turn the disc slightly and write the next letter of the name in the window. Do this for several names so that they appear on different parts of the disc. This is how a computer disc would store lots of names (though each letter would be in the form of an on-off code-number).

To read the disc, move the window to the right track and turn the disc. The letters of the name appear in the window as the disc turns. In a disc-drive, the head turns the magnetic signals into electric code signals. These go via the processor chip to RAM memory chips inside the computer.

A tape-player contains a reel or cassette of magnetic tape instead of a disc. The tape moves past the head to read and write the signals.

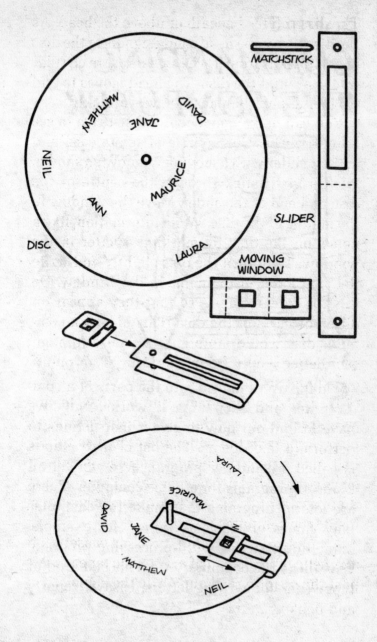

MATCHSTICK

SLIDER

MOVING
WINDOW

DISC

NEIL

ANN

MATTHEW

JANE

DAVID

MAURICE

LAURA

DAVID

JANE

MATTHEW

NEIL

MAURICE

LAURA

CHAPTER 5

COMMANDING THE COMPUTER

I WILL OBEY YOUR EVERY COMMAND

*S*o far we've looked into the parts of a computer and seen how it works. Now we have to find out how to give it instructions to perform a task for us. The list of instructions is called a computer program. We can get all kinds of programs for a home computer. There are lots of programs that make the computer play games or teach us things, for example. Many adults use a word-processing program. This turns the computer into a special kind of typewriter for writing letters, essays, reports and books.

The programs come on magnetic discs or tapes. The discs or tapes contain the instructions in the form of code signals. You operate the computer to 'load' the program from the disc or tape into the computer. The code signals then go to the computer's memory and the program is ready to start or 'run'.

FLOPPY (FLEXIBLE) DISC

TAPE REEL

TAPE CASSETTE

COMPUTER SPEAK

You can write your own computer programs. However, the computer needs instructions that are made up of lots of on-off code signals. It is very hard to work out instructions in this form, but you can use a computer language to write programs instead. The computer language has instructions in the form of words that you type on the computer's keyboard. The computer changes the words into the sets of code signals that it needs to work.

If you have a computer, it will probably use the computer language called BASIC. This language is quite easy to learn and use. Get permission, if necessary, to use the computer and set it up to write a program in BASIC. Ask an adult, or look at your computer manual if you do not know how to do this.

BASIC programs have lines of instructions. Each line has a number and then an instruction. The computer follows the lines in the order of their numbers to carry out the instructions, which are made of commands and variables. A command is an English word that makes the computer carry out a particular action. A variable is a code letter or set of letters that stands for a number or a word.

GREETINGS

We're going to write a simple four-line program using three commands and one variable. Type these lines on the computer. Press the key marked RETURN or ENTER at the end of each line. Line numbers normally go in tens. Note that the number 0 (zero) may appear as a nought with a line through it.

```
10 PRINT "ENTER YOUR NAME"
20 INPUT N$
30 PRINT "HELLO"; N$
40 GOTO 10
```

Run this program. If you do not know how to do this, use the manual or an adult will show you. The computer asks you to enter your name: type it on the keyboard and then press RETURN or ENTER. The computer says hello to you, and then starts again. To stop the program, press the key marked ESCAPE or BREAK.

Let's look at each line of the program to see how it works. The first line has the command PRINT. This instructs the computer to display something on the screen. The words to be displayed are placed between double quote marks ("). So as the computer reaches line 10, ENTER YOUR NAME appears on the screen.

Line 20 has the command INPUT followed by the variable N$ ($ is the dollar sign). This makes the computer wait until you have entered your name, and your name stays in the computer memory under the code N$. You can use any letter, but N is helpful because it stands for name. The dollar sign, which is called 'string', tells the computer to expect letters and not numbers.

INPUT IS LIKE GETTING INFORMATION NEEDED FOR A JOB

COMPUTER

PUT YOUR MESSAGE INTO BOX N$

N$

Line 30 makes the computer display HELLO followed by your name. PRINT commands it to display whatever is in double quotes followed by whatever is in the variable N$. It's called a variable because the name can vary from one person to another. The semicolon (;) makes the name appear next to HELLO.

Line 40 has the command GOTO followed by a number. This instructs the computer to go to the line with this number. As line 10 is the first line, the computer starts the program again.

GOTO IS LIKE JUMPING FROM ONE PART OF A JOB TO ANOTHER

COMPUTER

START AGAIN

If you want to keep a program, you can 'save' it. You give the program a name, and the computer stores the program on a disc or tape. You can then load the program back into the computer whenever you want to use it. The manual or an adult will show you how to save and load a program.

GETTING THE MESSAGE

You can alter this program to make it do something else. The manual or an adult will show you how to change or edit a program. Change line 30 to:

30 IF N$ = "JOHN" THEN PRINT "YOU ARE MY FRIEND"

Instead of JOHN, you can use the name of someone you know and get them to run the program. The computer will then say YOU ARE MY FRIEND (but you could change line 30 to make it display any other kind of message!). If the name is not JOHN (or whatever name you choose), then the computer starts again and asks for a new name.

Line 30 contains two new and important commands — IF and THEN. These enable the computer to make a decision. IF is followed by N$ = "JOHN". The computer looks to see if this is true or untrue. It checks whether the name in the variable N$ is in fact JOHN (or the name you choose) or not. If so, it continues to the next command in the line and displays YOU ARE MY FRIEND. If not, the computer ignores the rest of the line and goes to the next line in the program.

NIFTY NUMBERS
Now let's see how quickly the computer handles numbers. Try this program:

```
10 PRINT "ENTER A NUMBER"
20 INPUT N
30 FOR X = 1 TO 12
40 PRINT X; "TIMES"; N; "EQUALS"; X*N
50 NEXT
```

This program asks you for a number. Enter any number, and the computer instantly displays the multiplication table for that number. The variable N stands for number. It has no $ sign, so the computer expects a number and not letters.

Three more important commands appear in lines 30 and 50 – FOR, TO and NEXT. These make the computer go into a loop, which means

FOR NEXT IS LIKE REPEATING PART OF A JOB SEVERAL TIMES

KEEP PAINTING UNTIL THE MESSAGE IN BOX N SAYS 12

COMPUTER

that it goes round the part of the program between FOR and NEXT several times. As it does this, the variable X changes. It starts with the value before TO and ends with the value after TO. X therefore starts with a value of 1 and increases by 1 each time until its value reaches 12, so the program loops 12 times.

Line 40 displays the table. It shows the value of X, N and X*N (which is the value of X times the value of N). So if N is 2, on the third loop when X has reached 3, it displays 3 TIMES 2 EQUALS 6.

CHAPTER 6

PREPARING A PROGRAM

*I*t's not easy to write computer programs. You have to learn one or more computer languages, which contain many more commands than the few BASIC commands that you have already tried out. And a program like a good computer game will contain hundreds or thousands of instructions.

As people play the game, the computer will follow different paths through the program, depending on how the game goes. This means that the programmer who writes a program like a computer game has to think of all the possible ways that people will use the program. He or she must make sure that nothing will ever go wrong. Mistakes in a program are called 'bugs'. A program is tested to find any bugs and they are then removed from the program.

START WITH A CHART

Before writing a computer program, it is best to sit down and prepare the program. Think of the task that the program must perform. If it is a game, think of the rules of the game and work out all the steps that take place. Think about how people play, what happens when people win and lose, and how the score works. When you have got all these ideas clear, you can begin to change them into instructions for the computer.

One way to do this is to make a flow chart. This is a diagram that shows how the program will work. We can make a flow chart for a well-known game, and then change it into a BASIC program. The game is I Spy.

The first step is to start the game. The next

step is for a person to choose a letter, and then an object beginning with this letter. The person does not tell anyone else. To make a flow chart, you write down these steps and link them with arrows. So the first part of the chart would look like this:

Then the person asks people to guess the object, and they make a guess. If the guess is right, the person says so and the game ends. But if the guess is wrong, the person says it is wrong and the people have to guess again. The second part of the chart would look like this:

I SPY A PROGRAM

Now we have to change the flow chart into an I Spy program. We can do this with some of the commands used in Chapter 5, plus one extra command.

START in the flow chart is the same as running the program. The first line in the program will instruct the computer to display a message asking the person to enter a letter. Then the computer will wait for a letter to be put into a variable – say L$.

```
10 PRINT "ENTER A LETTER"
20 INPUT L$
```

Then the computer must ask the person to enter the name of an object beginning with the letter in L$. This is put into the variable O$.

```
30 PRINT "ENTER AN OBJECT
BEGINNING WITH"; L$
40 INPUT O$
```

The other people playing the game must not look at the screen while the person is choosing a letter and object. These will probably stay on the screen, so we must next clear the screen. On most computers, the command CLS does this. If it does not work on your computer, look in the manual to find out the command that clears the screen.

50 CLS

The computer must now display a message giving the letter and asking people to guess the object. Two PRINT commands split the message into two lines on the screen. The computer then waits for a guess, which is put into the variable G$.

```
60 PRINT "I SPY WITH MY LITTLE EYE"
70 PRINT "SOMETHING BEGINNING
WITH"; L$
80 INPUT G$
```

Now the computer must find out if the guess is the same as the object. If this is true, then the computer must jump to the end of the program, which we can put at a high line-number – say 200.

```
90 IF G$ = O$ THEN GOTO 200
```

If the guess is not the same as the object, the

computer goes to the next line in the program. This must tell people to try again. Then the computer must jump back in the program so that they can enter another guess.

```
100 PRINT "WRONG - TRY AGAIN"
110 GOTO 80
```

The last line says that the guess is right.

```
200 PRINT G$; "IS RIGHT"
```

The program stops here, and you would have to run it again to restart the game. So to make it start again automatically, add one more line:

```
210 GOTO 10
```

You can write programs to make your computer do all kinds of tasks. This book would have to be very big indeed to show you how to use all the commands in your computer. If you want to do more computer programming, you can find out more in your manual or in books that tell you how to program your computer.

CHAPTER 7

IT'S ALL DONE BY NUMBERS

TWO FAT LADIES, 88 — FOUR AND TWO, 42 —....

BINGO!

When we play a computer game, the machine can bombard us with words, pictures and music. It seems to behave like a writer, artist and musician all at once. Yet all the computer is doing inside is counting numbers very quickly. It turns the letters in words into code-numbers. A becomes 65 and B becomes 66, for example. The positions and colours of shapes in pictures are given numbers. The pitches and lengths of musical notes become numbers.

Why does the computer have to work with numbers? It is because the parts in a computer are electrical. When the computer works, electric signals flash to and fro among its many parts. These electric signals can be easily made to contain code-numbers.

COMPUTER CODE

However, the computer's code-numbers are not like the numbers that we use. Our numbers are decimal numbers. They have ten numerals – 0, 1, 2, 3, 4, 5, 6, 7, 8, and 9. We invented this system of numbers because we have ten fingers on our hands. A computer would not like this system – but not because it has no fingers. The reason is that decimal numbers are too complicated. The computer needs a much simpler system of numbers. It uses binary numbers, which have only two numerals – 0 and 1. The letter A becomes 01000001, which is the binary number for 65.

Why does the computer go to all the trouble of changing things into a code of binary numbers? The reason is that binary numbers can easily be turned into electric signals. The numbers become code signals made of pulses or bits of electricity moving along wires and through the parts in the computer. Each bit of electricity in a code signal can be either switched on or switched off. 0 in a number is

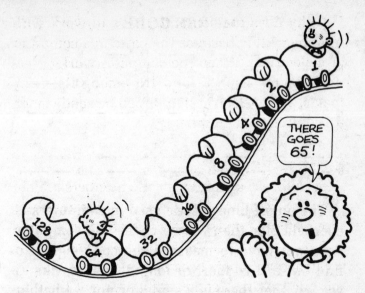

off, and 1 is on. So the code signal for A is off-on-off-off-off-off-off-on. As this code signal moves along a wire or through a part in the computer, the electricity goes off and on in this order.

DOTS AND DASHES

This kind of code is not new. Morse code is a similar kind of code for letters and numbers that is used for sending messages. It was invented 150 years ago. The code consists of short and long sounds or short and long flashes of light. You can send a Morse message by switching a torch on and off. Here is the code: a dot means a short flash or sound, and a dash means a long flash or sound.

MORSE CODE

A	·—	B	—···	C	—·—·	D	—··	E	·
F	··—·	G	——·	H	····	I	··	J	·———
K	—·—	L	·—··	M	——	N	—·	O	———
P	·——·	Q	——·—	R	·—·	S	···	T	—
U	··—	V	···—	W	·——	X	—··—	Y	—·——
Z	——··								

1	·————	2	··———	3	···——	4	····—	5	·····
6	—····	7	——···	8	———··	9	————·	0	—————

The on-off binary code used in computers is even simpler than Morse code. The computer does not have to measure the code signal to find out if it is short or long. It just checks to see whether there is a signal or not — whether the electricity is on or off. The difference between on and off is very clear, and the code signals flash between the many parts of the computer without the code-numbers going wrong.

BINARY ABACUS

Let's make an abacus to look at binary numbers. It's much simpler than the decimal abacus shown in Chapter 1. We can make one with a piece of stiff paper.

Cut four square windows in the paper, then fold it and stick the two edges together as shown. Cut out four strips of paper. Fix them so that they can slide up and down beneath the windows. Colour the strips with a red square marked 0, and a green square marked 1

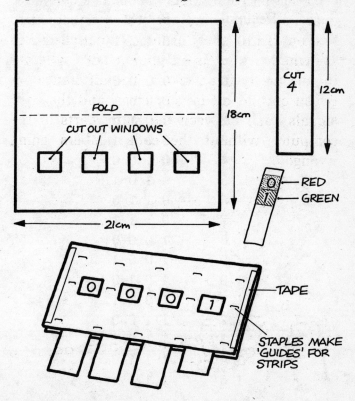

FOLD

CUT OUT WINDOWS

18cm

21cm

CUT 4

12cm

RED
GREEN

TAPE

STAPLES MAKE 'GUIDES' FOR STRIPS

as shown. Write 8, 4, 2 and 1 above the windows.

You can first use the abacus to change any decimal number up to 15 into a binary number. All you have to do is work out the combination of 8, 4, 2 and 1 that makes up the number. The number 11 is $8+2+1$, for example. So 11 becomes 1011, meaning 8–yes, 4–no, 2–yes, 1–yes. Move the strips to show 1011; the colours are green-red-green-green or on-off-on-on.

Decimal		Binary			
10	1	8	4	2	1
	0	0	0	0	0
	1	0	0	0	1
	2	0	0	1	0
	3	0	0	1	1
	4	0	1	0	0
	5	0	1	0	1
	6	0	1	1	0
	7	0	1	1	1
	8	1	0	0	0
	9	1	0	0	1
1	0	1	0	1	0
1	1	1	0	1	1
1	2	1	1	0	0
1	3	1	1	0	1
1	4	1	1	1	0
1	5	1	1	1	1

PUTTING THE BITS TOGETHER

The computer works by adding binary numbers together. We can do this with the binary abacus. There are four very simple rules to follow:

RULE A 0 AND 0 MAKE 0 AND CARRY 0
RULE B 0 AND 1 MAKE 1 AND CARRY 0
RULE C 1 AND 0 MAKE 1 AND CARRY 0
RULE D 1 AND 1 MAKE 0 AND CARRY 1

TEECHA

Let's add 4 and 5 using the binary abacus. 4 is 0100 and 5 is 0101. First set the abacus to 0100 (4). Now add 0101 (5). You add the four parts or bits of the number separately, starting with the bit at the right-hand end of the number (just as you do when you add decimal numbers). Add 1 to window 1. Rule B applies, giving 0101. Now add 0 to window 2. Rule A applies, and you get 0101. Next add 1 to window 4. Rule D applies and you carry 1 to window 8, giving 1001. Lastly add 0 to window 8. Rule C applies, giving 1001, which is the answer. This is $1 \times 8 + 0 \times 4 + 0 \times 2 + 1 \times 1$, which equals 9.

To subtract binary numbers, you do not need to learn any more rules. You do it by adding in the same way, and also by inverting, which is simply changing every 0 in a number to 1 and every 1 to 0. Let's subtract 6 from 13. First put 13 (1101) on the abacus. Then invert it to get 0010. Add 6 (0110) to get 1000. Lastly invert this result to get the answer – 0111 or 7.

Multiplying and dividing can be easy too. To multiply a binary number by 2, shift each bit one window to the left and make window 1 a 0. For example, 0011 (3) multiplied by 2 is 0110 (6). To divide by 2, shift each bit one window to the right and make window 8 a 0. 1110 (14) becomes 0111 (7).

In computing, the parts of binary numbers

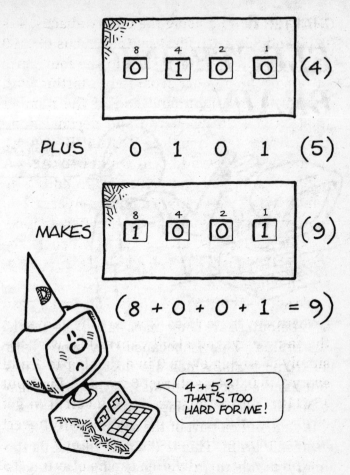

(4)

PLUS 0 1 0 1 (5)

MAKES (9)

$(8 + 0 + 0 + 1 = 9)$

4 + 5?
THAT'S TOO
HARD FOR ME!

(the 1s and 0s) are, in fact, called bits. Computing often uses familiar words in a different way. The word bit in computing is short for binary digit, which means a numeral in a binary number. However, you can still think of bits as the pieces of a binary number or bits of electricity in a code signal.

CHAPTER 8

ELECTRONIC BRAIN

IT'S GOT A CATERPILLAR FOR A BRAIN

*C*omputers are sometimes called 'electronic brains'. This is because they work with electronic parts, which are the kinds of parts that handle electric signals. As they also seem to be able to think, computers are like brains.

In fact, only a part of the computer is like an electronic brain. This is the part that adds the binary numbers in the code signals. It gets code signals from other parts of the computer, and also sends out code signals that control the rest of the computer. This part is really the brain of the computer. It's called the processor, because it processes or handles the signals. As it works, the processor follows strict rules and is totally logical in its operations.

Often the processor is known as a micro-processor. 'Micro' means small, so it's a small processor. A home computer is sometimes called a microcomputer, or just a 'micro', because it is a small computer. The processor is one of the microchips inside the computer. A microchip is made of a small chip or slice of a special electrical material called a semi-conductor. Inside the chip are thousands of very tiny electronic parts that handle the electric code signals.

ADDERS AND LADDERS

Let's see how the processor is able to add binary numbers together. This happens in a section of the processor called the adder. The code signals enter the adder. The bits – the

START

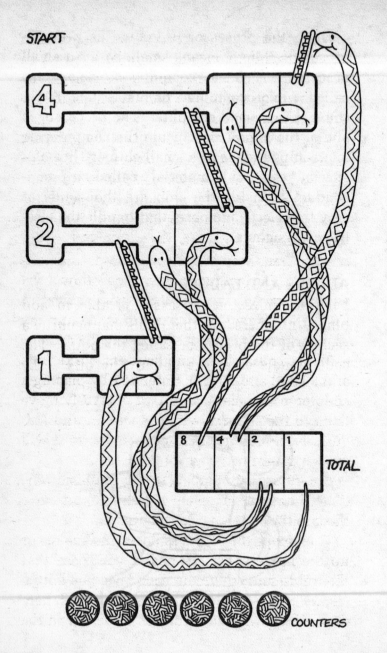

4

2

1

8 4 2 1

TOTAL

COUNTERS

72

on-off parts of the electric signals – are then added together using the four rules given in Chapter 7. The tiny electronic parts inside the adder change the bits so that a code signal for the result comes out.

You can see what happens by playing Adders and Ladders. It's rather like Snakes and Ladders. You need six counters. Play on the board on page 72, or photocopy this page and play on it. Using the counters, you enter two binary numbers at START. Each number has three bits. Each counter is an on-bit or 1. The counters then move down the snakes or up the ladders, and arrive at TOTAL. Moving the counters adds up the numbers and the result appears at TOTAL.

To see how Adders and Ladders works, let's add 5 (101) and 7 (111). Enter 101 by placing a counter on levels 4 and 1 at START. Move them to the squares with the snakes and ladders; each counter must move as far as it will go (see Diagram 1, page 74).

Enter the next number (111) in the same way. Place a counter on levels 4, 2 and 1, and move them to the squares (see Diagram 2).

Then move the counters down the snakes or up the ladders. On the board, you'll see that the right-hand square on each level has both a snake and a ladder. A counter placed here slides down the snake, unless a counter in the

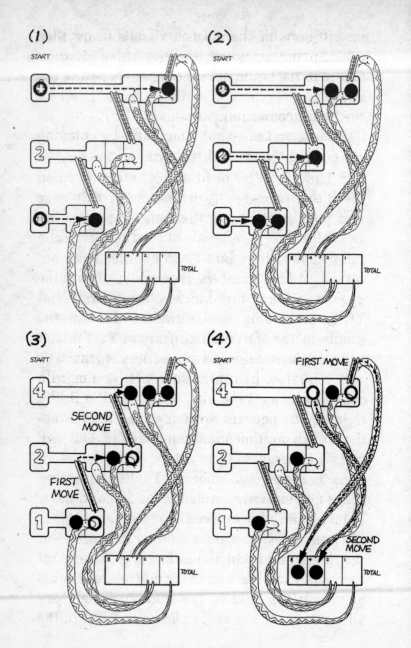

next square blocks it. In this case, the counter goes up the ladder to the next level. It then moves to the squares in the same way as at the start.

A counter in the next square always blocks the snake and does not move. A counter in the left square always slides down its snake.

Start on level 1. The first counter cannot slide down the snake, because the second counter is blocking it. So the first counter goes up the ladder to level 2, where it moves to the middle square. The second counter does not move.

Level 2 now has two counters. The counter in the middle square blocks the snake, so the first counter goes up the ladder to level 4 and moves to the left square. The counter in the middle square does not move (see Diagram 3).

Level 4 now has three counters. The middle counter blocks the snake, so the counter in the right square goes up the ladder and then down the snake to the square 8 in TOTAL. The middle counter does not move. The counter in the left square slides down its snake to square 4 in TOTAL. There are counters on 8 and 4 in TOTAL, so the answer is 1100 or 12 (see Diagram 4).

Adders and Ladders works for any three-bit numbers (numbers up to 7) and gives a four-bit result (up to 15). Try adding some more numbers.

CARRY ON COMPUTING

In a computer, bits of electricity move along wires in the same kind of way as the counters move up the ladders and down the snakes. The adder in a computer's processor has parts called half-adders, which are like the levels in our adder. Like us, computers add numbers by carrying one (see Chapter 1). Our adder is carrying one when a counter goes up a ladder to the next level. The processor carries one by sending a bit of electricity along a wire to the next half-adder. The next chapter tells you more about the parts inside the half-adder. You can find out how it makes the bits of electricity move so that the computer is able to add up numbers.

CHAPTER 9

THROUGH THE GATES

YOU'VE GOT A CLOCK — WHAT'S THE TIME

IT'S 101 TO 1011. YOU SHOULD BE IN BED!

*A*s a computer works, the electronic parts inside it make and change electric code signals. People first worked out how to put parts together to do this about fifty years ago. The very first computer was invented in Britain during the Second World War. Its task was to crack enemy code messages. The first computers were huge machines; some were as big as houses. This was because their parts were

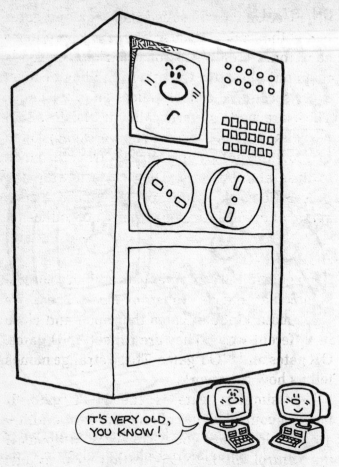

IT'S VERY OLD, YOU KNOW!

quite large. Since then, computer parts have been made smaller and smaller and many computers are now small machines.

The binary code signals in a computer are made of bits of electricity that move along wires from one part to another. Each code has a particular order in which the bits go on and off. Electronic parts called the clock and gates make the code signals. The clock produces short bursts or pulses of electricity. It sends them out one after the other, millions of them every second. The clock pulses go to the gates. These are made of parts called transistors that work like fast electric switches. The gates open to allow the pulses of electricity from the clock to pass along a wire. They close to stop the pulses. So as the gates open and close, a code signal of on-off bits of electricity is produced.

AND OR NOT

Each gate in the computer gets a binary control signal that makes it open or close. There are three main kinds of gates that open and close in different ways. They are called AND gates, OR gates and NOT gates. These strange names tell us how they work.

The simplest gate is the NOT gate. It needs a control signal of one off-bit or on-bit – a 0 or 1 in binary code – to work. It opens if the control bit is NOT 1 (that is 0 or off) and passes an electric pulse from the clock to give an on-bit (1). If the control bit is 1 (on), the gate closes to give an off-bit (0). So a NOT gate gets a 0 and sends out a 1, or it gets a 1 and sends out a 0. It inverts the binary number, changing 0s to 1s, and 1s to 0s.

The OR gate needs a control signal of two

bits to work. It opens if the first OR the second bit is 1 (or both are 1). It closes only if both control bits are 0. The AND gate also needs a control signal of two bits. It opens if the first bit AND the second bit are 1. If either or both control bits are 0, the gate closes.

AND GATE

0	AND	0	CLOSED
0	AND	1	CLOSED
1	AND	0	CLOSED
1	AND	1	OPEN

OR GATE

0	AND	0	CLOSED
0	AND	1	OPEN
1	AND	0	OPEN
1	AND	1	OPEN

NOT GATE

0	OPEN
1	CLOSED

GO   STOP

HALF-ADDER

The computer uses sets of gates to add binary numbers together. Inside the adder in the processor are several half-adders. Each one contains two AND gates, an OR gate and a NOT gate. The half-adder performs the four rules of binary addition given on page 67. It carries out just one stage of the addition and gets two bits, one from each number being added. It adds them to produce a total bit and a carry bit. The total bit goes to the result produced by the adder. The carry bit goes to the next half-adder, which carries out the next stage of the addition.

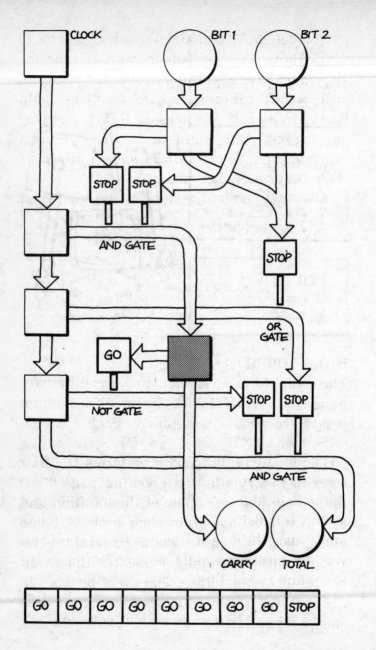

CLOCK BIT 1 BIT 2

STOP STOP

AND GATE

STOP

OR GATE

GO

NOT GATE STOP STOP

AND GATE

CARRY TOTAL

GO	GO	GO	GO	GO	GO	GO	GO	STOP

You can make a model like a board game to show how the half-adder works. Use the design on page 82, or photocopy this page and use it. Cut out nine square counters, eight marked GO and one marked STOP. Start by placing six GO counters in the five light squares and the CLOCK square. Put the STOP counter in the dark square.

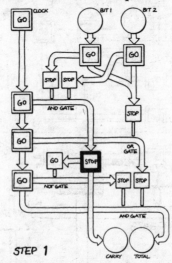

STEP 1

The counters are pulses or on-bits of electricity (1s in binary code). The paths are wires in the half-adder, and the STOP and GO signs are the transistors in the gates. As the counters move over the board, they move in the same way as electric signals flowing through the wires and transistors.

Place GO counters in the two BIT circles for the bits to be added together. Let's follow rule B and add 0 and 1. Place no counter (0) in the BIT 1 circle and a counter (1) in the BIT 2 circle. Now move the counters. Start with the BIT circles. One counter moves down from BIT 2, and meets a GO counter in a square.

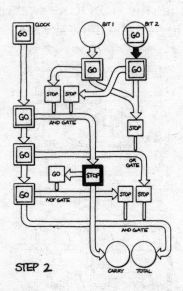

STEP 2

The counter in the square follows its path and goes to the top AND gate, changing one sign from STOP to GO. The first counter then continues to the OR gate, changing the STOP sign to GO (Step 3).

Now move the GO counter in the CLOCK square. When it meets a counter at a square, move both counters along both paths as before (Step 4).

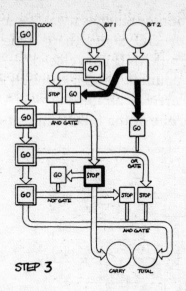

STEP 3

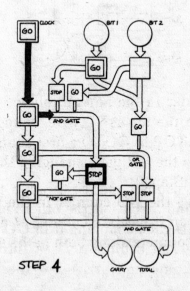

STEP 4

When a counter reaches a gate, it must obey the STOP or GO signs there. One counter will find the top AND gate closed.

The next counter passes through the open OR gate; it arrives at the bottom AND gate and changes one of the STOP signs to GO.

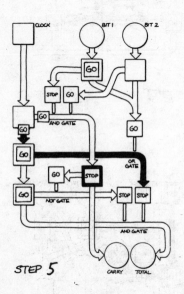

STEP 5

The next counter passes through the open NOT gate and arrives at the other sign in the bottom AND gate, changing it to GO (Step 6). Finally, the last counter passes through the open AND gate and arrives at the TOTAL

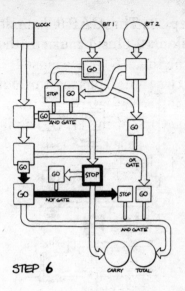

STEP 6

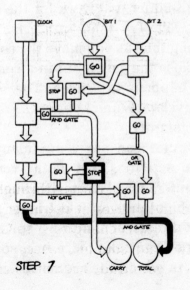

STEP 7

circle (Step 7). The CARRY circle is empty. This is rule B: 0 plus 1 make 1 (the total) and carry 0.

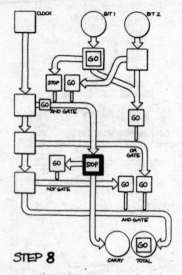

STEP 8

Our half-adder will work for the other three rules as well. Try them out. Each one takes quite a long time as you move the counters and open or close the gates. But in a computer, the addition happens in a flash. The bits of electricity travel very quickly and the gates open or close instantly.

A computer can carry out many different tasks and activities. Yet at the very heart of the computer, all of them become just rapid movements of bits of electricity performing simple additions at lightning speed. Millions of additions can take place in a second. Only the order in which the sequences of additions take place makes one task or activity different from another. So, wonderful though the computer may seem, it is really nothing more than a super-fast adding-machine.

INDEX

More Young Puffin Fact Books

TUNE IN – How TV and radio work
Neil Ardley

How can a TV set pick up sound and pictures from thin air? Another book in which you can find out for yourself with the clear and fascinating descriptions of simple experiments which vividly explain the principles of TV and radio.

SNAP HAPPY – How a camera takes pictures
Neil Ardley

Lenses, films, shutters, flash – what are they and how do they enable a camera to take photos? Taking photos with modern cameras is very easy, but have you ever wondered how they work? Although the most expensive ones can seem very complex, this book describes simple activities using household items which vividly demonstrate the basics of what happens in a camera.

WINGS AND THINGS – How an aircraft flies
Neil Ardley

Airliners, fighter-planes, helicopters, balloons, hang-gliders – how is it possible for them to get off the ground, let alone stay in the air for long periods of time? Using readily available inexpensive items, these activities vividly illustrate the basic scientific principles underlying one of the major technological adventures of the twentieth century.

WATCH OUT! Keeping safe outdoors
Rosie Leyden and Suzanne Ahwai

A book to give children an awareness of the dangers lurking outside on the roads, on their bikes, near water, on building sites, etc. It is full of fun, puzzles and quizzes as well as being packed with information to help keep them safe.

PICK OF THE PETS – From bugs to bunnies
Penny Lloyd

A fun book in which children can find out all about a variety of pets, big and small – how to look after them, how to play with them and discover some amazing facts about them.

EUREKA!
Chris Meade

Facts and fun on science, natural history, transport and ecology, with information on where to find out more. Published in co-operation with the Museums Association.

EUROPE UP AND AWAY!
Sue Finnie

A lively book packed with information about Western Europe which includes sections on stamps, car numbers and language as well as topics related to an individual country (from Flamenco dancing to Frogs' Legs!)